RETAIL RESCUE

*Real Leadership
in a Retail World
That's Lost Its Way*

ANDREW J DIMIO

ISBN:979-8-9990579-0-7

Printed in the United States of America.

For every retail employee who deserved a better leader—
and every manager who wants to be one.

Contents

Introduction   1

PART I: THE PROBLEM WITH MODERN RETAIL LEADERSHIP

Chapter 1
The Day I Knew I Would Never Manage Like That Again   5

Chapter 2
Toxic Bosses, Narcissists & the Slow Death of Morale   8

Chapter 3
Are You Leading, or Just Demanding?   11

Chapter 4
When Your Team Stops Trying: How Burnout Begins   15

Chapter 5
The Myth of the Natural Retail Rockstar   18

Chapter 6
Culture Isn't Free Snacks, It's Consistency   21

Chapter 7
Feedback Is Not a Weapon   24

Chapter 8
What You Allow, You Endorse   28

Chapter 9
You Can't Coach What You Don't Observe   31

Chapter 10
Leadership Without Ego   35

Chapter 11
How to Handle Being Wrong in Front of Your Team   38

PART II: FIXING THE FLOOR

Chapter 12
Why Folding Tables Matter More Than You Think 45

Chapter 13
Visual Merchandising: The Silent Salesperson 48

Chapter 14
Your Staff Isn't Lazy—They're Undertrained 51

Chapter 15
Clienteling Starts with Trust, Not Scripts 54

Chapter 16
Training Is Not One and Done 58

Chapter 17
What Gets Scheduled Gets Done 61

Chapter 18
The Backstock Is the Truth 65

Chapter 19
The Leader Who Takes the Bad Shift 69

PART III: BUILDING A TEAM THAT WORKS WITHOUT YOU

Chapter 20
The Manager's Real Job: Build Other Managers 75

Chapter 21
Servant Leadership on the Sales Floor 78

Chapter 22
You Don't Need to Be Feared to Be Respected 83

Chapter 23
How to Create a Culture of Ownership 87

Chapter 24
Coaching vs. Correcting: Know the Difference 92

Chapter 25
Mentoring Employees Who Might Outgrow You   96

Chapter 26
Holding the Line Without Burning Bridges   100

Chapter 27
The Wrong Hire Can Undo It All   105

PART IV: THE SELF-AWARE LEADER

Chapter 28
You're Not Too Busy—You're Disorganized   111

Chapter 29
You Can't Be a Great Leader If You're Running on Empty   115

PART V: SCALING & LEGACY

Chapter 30
The Exit Plan – Leading So You Can Step Away   121

Chapter 31
Leaving It Better Than You Found It   125

Introduction

I still remember the day I broke.

I was sitting on a patio chair outside the shop, hands shaking, phone in my lap, reading a text message that ended with:
"If you can't get this done, I won't pay you for the day."

It was a list of tasks impossible to complete in an 8-hour shift. Not challenging—impossible. And the threat wasn't just about money. It was about power, control, and the kind of leadership that crushes people instead of building them.

I cried that day. Alone. On a patio chair.
And I walked out.

That was the day I stopped believing in bosses—and started believing in leadership.

$$\bullet \quad \bullet \quad \bullet \quad \bullet \quad \bullet$$

This isn't a book written from a boardroom.
This is written from the backstock. From behind the register. From the fitting room. From all the places real retail happens.

I've worked for narcissists who used fear as their management style.
I've worked for control freaks who rewarded loyalty with micromanagement.
I've been underpaid, undervalued, and talked down to while building million-dollar stores for people who never said thank you.

And I've also worked for the best boss I've ever known—someone we lovingly called "Yoda" because she was short and all-knowing. She showed me what real mentorship looked like. She folded shirts beside us. She coached first and critiqued second. She didn't just say we were the future of the company—she trained us like we already were.

So I've seen both sides.

This book is about making sure more people become Yodas—and fewer become the bosses we still carry baggage from.

$$\bullet \quad \bullet \quad \bullet \quad \bullet \quad \bullet$$

If you've worked in retail long enough, you've seen the same stories repeat:
Good employees quit not because of the job, but because of the person above them.
Customers leave not because the product was wrong—but because the culture was off.
And stores underperform not because of lazy staff—but because of disorganized leadership.

Leadership is not about barked orders, ego, or being feared.
Leadership is how you show up every day—especially when things go wrong.
It's how you build, train, and lead a team that could function even if you weren't there.

That's what I call *Retail Rescue.*

$$\bullet \quad \bullet \quad \bullet \quad \bullet \quad \bullet$$

This book is for the store managers who still care.
For the assistant managers who want to do better than what they were shown.
For the owners who want a team they don't have to babysit.
And for anyone who's ever walked into work and said, *"There has to be a better way to do this."*

There is.

And this book will show you how.

Let's start with the moment it all shifted:

PART I
The Problem with Modern Retail Leadership

This section uncovers what's broken—
how poor leadership creates chaos, apathy, and burnout.

CHAPTER 1
The Day I Knew I Would Never Manage Like That Again

The worst moment of my retail career didn't happen during a customer meltdown.
It wasn't a failed launch or a sales goal I missed.

It was sitting outside a store—alone, on a metal patio chair—tears in my eyes, holding my phone in my hands, reading a message from my boss that said:

"If you can't complete this list, I won't pay you for the day."

I stared at that text while my heart pounded.

Not because I feared losing the money—though I needed it.
Not because the list was hard—though it was laughably impossible.
But because **that message summed up everything wrong with how people are treated in this industry**.

I wasn't new to retail. I knew hard work. I'd stayed late. Trained teams. Pulled visual flips with no help. I wasn't afraid of pressure.

But this was different.

This boss—let's call them Boss C—was the kind of leader who managed through **fear and instability.**
One moment they were cold and silent. The next, they were explosive and accusatory. There was no middle. No consistency. No humanity.

They expected miracles, gave no feedback, and used money, hours, and job security as bargaining chips.

That day's list included a full floor move, visual reset, product pulls, and backstock reorganization—all for one person to complete. In one shift. Without help. Without warning. With customers still coming through the doors.

And then the threat: *"No pay if it's not done."*

It broke something in me.

I'd never felt so disposable. So unseen. So angry and helpless at the same time.

• • • • •

That moment—sitting in that chair, completely burned out—was when I made myself a promise:

"If I ever manage people, I will never make them feel like this."

It became the filter I applied to every decision after that.

Was I pushing or supporting?
Was I training or blaming?
Was I building someone up—or just trying to "get through the day"?

Boss C wasn't just a bad manager. They were a turning point.
They forced me to confront what kind of leader I was becoming—and what kind I refused to be.

• • • • •

The truth is, most of us who get into leadership do so with good intentions. We want to help. We want to grow. We want to succeed.
But if we don't break the cycles we've been handed—if we don't question the environments we were shaped by—**we risk becoming the very people who broke us.**

That's what *Retail Rescue* is about.

It's not a rant. It's not a victim story.

It's a rebuild.

For the managers who care.
For the owners who've lost touch.
For the leaders who've felt that same chair beneath them, wondering how it all got this bad.

· · · · ·

If that's you—if you've felt the burnout, the pressure, the shame, the silence—then I promise: there's another way to do this.

There's a way to lead that builds trust, drives performance, and still allows people to be human.

I found it the hard way.
You don't have to.

Let's go.

CHAPTER 2

Toxic Bosses, Narcissists & the Slow Death of Morale

They yelled—loud, aggressive, and always too close.
They cursed like punctuation.
And any idea that wasn't their own was treated as a threat.

That was Boss D.
The owner.
And I was their #2.

When people talk about toxic work environments, they often picture something passive—silent tension, lack of communication, poor policies. But this wasn't that.
This was open, loud, ego-driven abuse. It was control masked as passion. Fear disguised as standards.

And the worst part?
It worked—until it didn't.

• • • • •

For a while, I convinced myself it was just their personality. That maybe this is what ownership had to look like. That maybe I was too soft.

But over time, I watched it destroy every single layer of morale in the business.

Employees stopped offering ideas.
Managers stopped asking questions.
Everyone walked on eggshells, trying not to set them off.
And behind the scenes, the whisper networks grew—people venting, job hunting, doing just enough to survive the week.

It wasn't a team anymore. It was a group of individuals trying not to get yelled at.

· · · · ·

Toxic leadership isn't just about how loud someone is. It's about what their presence *takes away* from the room.

With Boss D, the price was trust, creativity, and psychological safety.

Everything had to go through them.
Even basic operational ideas were treated as disloyalty.
If you suggested a new system, you were undermining their authority.
If you asked to fix a broken process, you were labeled negative.

Over time, no one spoke up at all.

And that's how morale dies—not overnight, but inch by inch, under the weight of someone else's insecurity.

· · · · ·

Here's the part most people don't understand:
Toxic bosses don't just damage performance. They damage **belief**.

People stop believing in the company.
They stop believing their voice matters.
Eventually, they stop believing in *themselves*.

That's what narcissistic leadership does—it shrinks the world down to one person's ego and expects everyone else to orbit around it.

And it's why good people leave. Not because they're soft. Not because they can't handle pressure.
But because they know staying would mean slowly becoming someone they don't want to be.

· · · · ·

I stayed longer than I should have.

Tried harder than most would.

I wanted to believe I could make a difference—that my presence would soften the sharp edges.

But in a culture built around ego, compassion becomes a liability.

So I left.

Not just for myself, but for the kind of leader I wanted to become.

And the kind of leader I refused to become.

•   •   •   •   •

If you're reading this and thinking of your own Boss D—you're not alone.

And if you've caught glimpses of that behavior in your own leadership—good.

That means you're self-aware enough to change it.

Toxic bosses aren't just bad for business. They're bad for the soul of the store.

And leadership that kills morale?

Isn't leadership at all.

CHAPTER 3
Are You Leading, or Just Demanding?

There's a difference between **having authority** and **being a leader**—but in retail, the two get confused far too often.

You're in charge of the schedule.
You have the keys.
You tell people what to do.
So you're a leader... right?

Not necessarily.

Telling someone what to do isn't leadership.
Expecting results without investment isn't leadership.
Correcting without teaching? Definitely not leadership.

That's just demanding.
And there's a big difference.

• • • • •

I've seen a lot of demanding managers.
I've even slipped into that mode myself early in my career—when I was tired, under pressure, and honestly didn't know any better.

You start with a team that needs direction, and it feels easier to just give orders.
You think, *"Why can't they just do it?"*
You assume laziness instead of looking at your own clarity.
And little by little, you stop leading—and start managing from frustration.

It's common. It's natural. And it's also correctable.

But only if you're willing to look at yourself first.

•　•　•　•　•

That's where the real work starts. **Self-awareness is the foundation of leadership.**

You have to ask hard questions:

- Am I clear with my expectations—or just reactive?
- Do I give people the tools to succeed—or just criticize when they fail?
- Am I invested in their growth—or just in my own convenience?

Demanding managers focus on tasks.
Leaders focus on people.

•　•　•　•　•

Here's what I've learned over the years:

- The more **present** you are, the less your team second-guesses themselves
- The more you **coach**, the less you have to correct
- The more you **model**, the less you have to enforce

When you lead well, your team starts to internalize the standard.
They want to get it right—not because they're afraid, but because they feel *part of something.*

And that's the difference.

•　•　•　•　•

I once had a manager who expected perfection in visuals—but never lifted a finger to train us.
They'd walk through the store in the morning and bark corrections. Not explanations. Not guidance. Just *"Fix this. Why is this still here? This looks awful."*

So we started doing just enough to avoid hearing from them.

No one wanted to take initiative.
No one wanted to get "creative."
We didn't care about improvement—we cared about not getting chewed out.

That's what demanding does. It creates compliance, not commitment.

· · · · ·

Contrast that with a time I trained a brand-new associate on fitting room standards.

I didn't just tell them what needed to be done. I walked the process with them.
I explained *why* it mattered—how speed there affected sales, customer perception, even shrink.
I made sure they saw the store from the customer's view.

And I came back later—not to check up, but to **reaffirm and coach**.

You know what happened?

They got fast. They got good. And they started training other people the same way.
Because leadership spreads. So does the lack of it.

· · · · ·

This chapter is the gut check.

If your team isn't performing the way you want—don't start with blame.
Start with the mirror.

Ask yourself:
Am I really leading? Or just demanding?

Because when you shift from commands to coaching...
From control to clarity...
From fear to trust...

You stop babysitting.
You start building.

And that's the kind of store people want to work in—and stay in.

CHAPTER 4
When Your Team Stops Trying: How Burnout Begins

Burnout doesn't always look like someone crying in the back room.
Sometimes it looks like someone doing the bare minimum.
Or clocking in silently.
Or responding with *"Okay."* instead of ideas.

It's not always dramatic.
More often—it's quiet.

And one of the fastest ways to burn out a team?
Micromanage them until they stop thinking for themselves.

• • • • •

Micromanagement doesn't just slow people down—it shuts them down.

When everything has to be approved, double-checked, or cleared by a manager, people stop taking initiative.
They stop noticing problems.
They stop fixing things on their own.
And eventually—they stop caring.

Not because they're lazy.
Not because they're unqualified.
But because the message has been made painfully clear:

"We don't trust you."

• • • • •

I've seen it happen in stores where the manager was always watching, always correcting, always redoing things that didn't match their exact personal preference.

At first, the team tried to get ahead—tried to solve problems on their own.

But after being micromanaged into the ground, they started waiting to be told what to do.
They only did the task they were assigned.
And they avoided the grey areas—the small moments of judgment and decision-making—because they were tired of doing things "wrong" in someone else's eyes.

So things started slipping.
Little things. Obvious things.
The kind of problems they *used* to fix on their own.

And that's when burnout starts—not because of workload, but because of **wasted effort and constant correction.**

• • • • •

Here's the part leaders often miss:

Burnout isn't just about working hard.
It's about working hard and still feeling like it's never good enough.

If someone's effort is always questioned...
If their decisions are always undone...
If their independence is treated like rebellion...

They will eventually shut down.

They'll stop bringing ideas.
They'll stop pushing forward.
And they'll stop trusting you.

• • • • •

Real leadership doesn't mean you let go completely.
It means you coach and release.
You train well, then step back.
You trust people to grow—even if they stumble a little along the way.

Because autonomy isn't just about freedom.
It's about respect.

And when people feel respected?
They perform better.
They catch the details.
They solve problems before you even hear about them.

· · · · ·

If your team seems checked out...
If mistakes keep happening that "should be obvious"...
If no one steps up unless you're watching...

You might not have a lazy team.
You might have a micromanaged one.

· · · · ·

Burnout doesn't come from effort alone.
It comes from effort without impact.
From work without trust.
From pressure without support.

So if your store feels heavy right now—if your team looks like they've stopped trying—ask yourself:

Have I created a space where they're allowed to think, act, and grow?

Or have I trained them to wait, react, and stay small?

CHAPTER 5
The Myth of the Natural Retail Rockstar

There's a myth in retail that some people are just "built for it."

They walk faster. Talk sharper. Learn quicker.

They can fold a wall, sell a full outfit, restock denim, and coach a new hire all before lunch.

And if you're not that?

If you're slower, quieter, less confident?

You must not be cut out for the job.

But here's the truth: most of those so-called naturals? They weren't born that way. They were led that way.

· · · · ·

I wasn't a natural.

I wasn't loud. I wasn't pushy. I wasn't someone who came in on Day 1 commanding the floor.

But I had something many don't get—I had someone who took the time to invest in me.

Boss B didn't just train me—they guided me.

They asked questions, listened to answers, and made me feel like it was safe to try—even if I got it wrong.

They didn't just correct—they taught.

They didn't just expect—they explained.

And they didn't just tell me I had potential—they gave me space to grow into it.

Looking back, that made all the difference.

• • • • •

So many people in retail never get that shot.

They're thrown in, given two rushed shifts, and expected to thrive.

When they don't immediately excel, they're labeled "not a fit."

And when they start doubting themselves, it's framed as a lack of drive—rather than a lack of support.

That's not just unfair. It's bad leadership.

You can't blame someone for what they were never taught.

You can't expect ownership from someone who was never invited to care.

• • • • •

The myth of the retail rockstar keeps us from seeing what's really missing:

Time. Coaching. Patience. Feedback. Trust.

People don't become rockstars on their own.

They're made through repetition, encouragement, and a system that values development over immediate perfection.

The best floor leads, key holders, and managers I've worked with weren't always the strongest on day one.

But they got there—because someone believed they could.

And someone led them like they already would.

• • • • •

If you're leading a team right now, and you're frustrated that no one is "stepping up," ask yourself:

- Have I created a space where they're allowed to?
- Have I shown them what "great" looks like—clearly, not just critically?
- Have I made it safe for them to ask questions, stumble, and improve?

Because if not, the issue might not be talent.

It might be opportunity.

• • • • •

When you let go of the myth, you start seeing potential everywhere.

Not just in the loudest voice, the flashiest seller, or the most confident applicant.

But in the ones watching closely. Practicing quietly. Waiting for a real leader to notice.

So if you weren't a natural? Neither was I.

We were just lucky enough to be led.

Now it's our turn to do the same.

How to Spot Quiet Potential

- They ask thoughtful questions instead of showing off
- They show up early, stay late, and rarely complain
- They take notes and remember what you say
- They watch how things work before jumping in
- They do the small things right, even when no one is watching
- They listen more than they speak—and learn fast when trusted

These are the ones who rise—if someone's willing to lead them there.

CHAPTER 6
Culture Isn't Free Snacks, It's Consistency

Culture is one of the most overused—and most misunderstood—words in modern retail.

Everyone says they want a "great store culture."

Teamwork, energy, positivity, trust.

So they plan a pizza party.

Bring in donuts.

Maybe throw in a casual dress Friday.

That's not culture.

That's a treat.

Culture isn't what you do once in a while.

It's what you allow, correct, reward, and repeat—every single day.

• • • • •

Here's what culture really is:
- If you let people show up late without consequences, you've created a culture of lateness.
- If you praise initiative and coach mistakes, you've created a culture of growth.
- If you correct in front of customers, play favorites, or disappear when it's hard, you've created a culture of fear or inconsistency.

Your culture is not what you say on the mission statement.

It's what your team experiences when you're not in the room.

● ● ● ● ●

The best cultures I've worked in weren't loud.

They weren't always the most social.

But they were steady. They were clear. And they were fair.

People knew the standard.

People trusted the process.

And people believed that leadership had their back.

That doesn't happen with cupcakes. It happens with consistency.

● ● ● ● ●

I once worked in a store where the culture shifted constantly—depending on the mood of the boss.

One day, they were your biggest cheerleader. The next, they were tearing into someone for a minor mistake.

We never knew what version of them we were getting.

So we stopped caring. We just tried to stay out of the way.

The job became survival.

And the culture became silence.

● ● ● ● ●

So here's the real question:

What happens in your store when you're not there?

If people cut corners the moment you leave—your culture is performative.

If they keep it clean, support each other, and self-correct—you've built something real.

That doesn't come from one great meeting.

It comes from a hundred moments of clarity, accountability, and follow-through.

• • • • •

A strong culture feels like this:
- Everyone knows what great looks like—and believes they can reach it
- Feedback is normal, not personal
- People step up without being asked
- New hires get trained the same way every time
- Bad behavior is addressed—not ignored
- The standard is the same on a busy Saturday as it is on a slow Tuesday

That's leadership.

And that's how culture sticks.

• • • • •

Snacks are nice.

Team lunches matter.

Celebrations are great.

But if you want real culture?

Show up. Stay consistent. Set the tone. Keep the promise.

The rest takes care of itself.

CHAPTER 7
Feedback Is Not a Weapon

Feedback is one of the most powerful tools in retail leadership.

It can build confidence.

Shape behavior.

Develop skills.

But too often, it's used the wrong way.

It becomes a punishment.

A performance.

Or worse—a passive-aggressive substitute for actual coaching.

And when that happens, feedback stops being helpful.

It becomes a weapon.

•   •   •   •   •

I've worked in stores where "feedback" was code for being called out—publicly, sarcastically, or under the guise of "just being honest."

I've seen managers correct someone in front of a customer, then wonder why that employee shut down the rest of the day.

I've seen associates coached for things they were never trained on.

And I've seen entire teams grow defensive, guarded, and disengaged—not because they didn't want to improve, but because they didn't trust the way improvement was handled.

· · · · ·

Here's the thing:
- Feedback that's unclear = confusing
- Feedback that's delayed = disconnected
- Feedback that's emotional = unsafe
- Feedback that's public = humiliating

If you want your team to grow, they need to know three things:
1. What's expected
2. How they're doing
3. That you're in their corner—even when something needs to change

· · · · ·

Over the years, I developed one of the most effective feedback tools I've ever used—and I built it from scratch based on what I wished I had early on.

The Self-Realization Coaching Session

Before a new hire ever hits the floor, I let them know these short coaching check-ins will happen.

Sometimes randomly. Sometimes tied to something I observed.

But always with the same goal: growth—not discipline.

I start each session with two simple questions:
- "What is something that you feel you did well in that sale?"
- "What is something that you feel you could have done better with?"

This does two things:
- It encourages self-awareness and accountability
- It makes feedback feel like a conversation, not a confrontation

And once they've answered, I share my own observations—not to correct them, but to support their growth.

"I agree with what you said about greeting quickly—that was strong. I also thought the way you recommended the upsell item was subtle and effective."

"One thing I noticed: you let them lead the conversation the entire time, which lost some control over the sale. Let's work on asking a few more qualifying questions next time."

They're heard.

They're guided.

And they walk away better than they came in.

That's coaching.

Not criticism.

· · · · ·

Compare that to weaponized feedback:
- "Really? This again?"
- "Did no one train you?"
- "This is why I can't leave anything to you."
- Delivered with a sigh, an eye roll, or sarcasm in front of others.

Even if the message is technically right, the delivery ensures no one hears it.

Because people don't just absorb what you say—they internalize how you say it.

· · · · ·

If your team seems resistant to coaching, ask yourself:
- Have I built trust first?
- Do I correct in private, not public?
- Do I acknowledge effort—not just errors?

- Do I invite reflection—or just deliver verdicts?

Feedback without trust is just noise.

Feedback with trust becomes growth.

• • • • •

So if you want your team to receive it better, start with how you give it.

- Be consistent
- Be private
- Be calm
- Be honest
- Be human

Because at the end of the day:

Feedback is a tool. Not a threat.

Use it to build—not break.

CHAPTER 8
What You Allow, You Endorse

Let's be clear:
Silence is permission.

Every time you let something slide—lateness, tone, missed tasks, cutting corners—you're not just "being patient."

You're *teaching your team what's okay.*

You may think, *"It's not worth making a scene."*
Or, *"They'll fix it on their own."*
Or, *"It's just this one time."*

But the moment you let a broken standard pass without correction?

You endorse it.

• • • • •

Leadership isn't just what you say.
It's what you *allow*.

And over time, the gap between what you *expect* and what you *enforce* becomes your real culture.

Not your mission statement.
Not your sales goals.
Not your "expectations" meeting.

Your culture is built in those quiet moments where you decide whether or not to step in.

• • • • •

Here's what this looks like in action:

- You expect fitting rooms to be recovered every 30 minutes, but no one checks.
- You say "teamwork matters," but let one person slack off every shift.
- You have a cell phone policy, but it's only enforced when upper management's around.
- You claim you care about development, but never follow up with the undertrained employee.

Eventually, the team stops listening to your words.

They start watching what you let slide.

• • • • •

This isn't about becoming militant.
It's about being *consistent*.

Consistency doesn't mean perfection.
It means **every team member knows the standard—and knows you'll hold it.**

"Your silence becomes someone else's excuse."
If you don't speak up, they assume it's fine.
If you don't follow up, they assume you didn't mean it.
And if you don't hold the line, they'll eventually stop respecting it.

• • • • •

How Leaders Accidentally Endorse the Wrong Things

- Avoiding tough conversations to keep the peace
- "Choosing your battles" a little too often
- Making exceptions for high performers
- Letting tone or attitude go unchecked because someone "gets results"

- Telling yourself "it's not a big deal today" over and over again

Each time this happens, the culture erodes.
Not instantly—but steadily.

And eventually, you wake up in a store you don't recognize.

·　·　·　·　·

You're not going to catch everything.
You're not going to fix every problem instantly.
But when you *do* see something, you need to act—*even if it's just a 30-second reset.*

Because what you allow *this week* becomes what's expected *next week*.

And once that bar drops, getting it back up is a much harder climb.

·　·　·　·　·

If Chapter 11 is about **showing up**,
this chapter is about **following through.**

Your presence builds visibility.
Your action builds credibility.

And your consistency builds culture.

CHAPTER 9
You Can't Coach What You Don't Observe

Coaching isn't something you do once a quarter.

It's not a form to fill out.

It's not a checkmark in your leadership binder.

Coaching is active. Daily. Intentional.

And to do it right, you have to be **there.**

"Inspect what you expect."

If you've communicated a standard—but never followed up to see it in action—you're not coaching. You're assuming.

• • • • •

You cannot lead from the office.

You cannot lead from the camera feed.

You cannot lead off a weekly report.

You can only lead what you observe—*in real time, on the floor, with the team.*

If you're not around, you're not developing anyone.

You're just maintaining. Maybe.

And that's not leadership. That's babysitting a system you didn't build.

• • • • •

Here's what happens when managers disappear into the backroom:

- Training becomes hearsay
- Feedback becomes guesswork

- Problems get missed until they become disasters
- Bad habits take root
- And new hires never know what "great" looks like in action

Meanwhile, the team starts to feel like no one notices, no one supports, and no one cares.

· · · · ·

One of the most powerful shifts I ever made as a leader was **staying visible**.

Not hovering. Not micromanaging.
Just *being there*—with intention.

Walking the floor.
Observing patterns.
Watching the conversations.
Seeing the sale happen.
Seeing the one that didn't.

And *then* coaching—not from assumption, but from experience.

· · · · ·

You can't correct the sales pitch if you didn't hear it.
You can't praise the upsell if you missed it.
You can't guide the new hire if you weren't watching their process.

So if you find yourself frustrated with how your team is performing, ask first:

"Have I actually seen them do it, or am I guessing based on results?"

· · · · ·

"Inspect what you expect."

You want clean tables? Walk the floor.
You want better service? Listen to how they greet.

You want stronger product knowledge? Ask them what they're recommending—and why.

Don't just tell them what you want.
Show up, see it, and guide them there.

• • • • •

Here's how strong leaders stay present without micromanaging:
- Ask to shadow for 5 minutes—then debrief with praise and 1 piece of coaching
- Pick one coaching theme for the week (greeting, upselling, handling objections)
- Use open-ended questions:
  - "What did you notice about that interaction?"
  - "What would you try differently next time?"
  - "How did that feel to you?"
- Acknowledge effort just as much as outcome

And don't save it all for later—*coach in the moment.*
That's when it sticks.

• • • • •

The Risk of Coaching from Reports
- **You're solving symptoms, not causes.** Reports show *results*, not *how* they happened.
- **You miss context.** A low UPT might come from handling a difficult customer perfectly.
- **You reinforce fear.** If coaching always comes after reports drop, feedback feels punitive—not helpful.
- **You lose accuracy.** Data can be incomplete, delayed, or misinterpreted.
- **You stop being seen.** When the team only sees you during reporting cycles, they stop seeing you as a partner.

Reports should confirm what you already saw—not replace it.

• • • • •

A clipboard won't build your team.
A floor presence will.

Because the best teams aren't just told what to do.

They're **shown, coached, encouraged, and seen.**

CHAPTER 10
Leadership Without Ego

The store isn't about you.

The team's energy?
Not about you.

The wins, the challenges, the bad reviews, the sudden walkouts, the surprise 20K Saturday?

Still—not about you.

And the moment you start making it about yourself, your ego will cloud every decision, every conversation, and every ounce of culture you're trying to build.

• • • • •

Leadership without ego isn't about pretending you don't matter.
It's about **knowing your impact—and choosing to center others anyway.**

Because when ego takes over:
- You stop listening
- You stop adapting
- You stop developing others
- And you start performing for approval instead of leading with purpose

• • • • •

Here's what ego in retail leadership often looks like:
- Needing to be right—even when you're wrong
- Downplaying feedback

- Avoiding delegation
- Taking credit for team wins
- Blaming others for misses
- Making decisions based on personal comfort instead of team clarity

You might still hit your numbers.
But you'll lose your people.

• • • • •

The best leaders I've ever known were confident—but grounded.
They had nothing to prove, because they knew the job wasn't about being *the boss*.
It was about building something bigger than themselves.

They didn't chase the spotlight.
They used it to highlight others.

And they didn't crumble when a mistake was theirs—they owned it, corrected it, and moved on.

That's strength.
And that's what leadership without ego feels like in practice.

• • • • •

Signs You're Leading With Ego (Even If You Don't Mean To)

- You shut down when challenged
- You struggle to say "I don't know"
- You take things personally when someone asks for feedback
- You talk more than you listen in 1:1s
- You're hesitant to develop others because "they might leave"

None of this makes you a bad leader.
It makes you a human one.

The key is recognizing it—and **choosing humility** when ego wants the mic.

$$\bullet \quad \bullet \quad \bullet \quad \bullet \quad \bullet$$

As Vic Keller says:

"The most impactful leaders I've met lead with humility, lift others up, and don't fear being surpassed—they expect it."

Your job isn't to be the smartest in the room.
It's to create a room where everyone else can grow smarter, more confident, and more capable.

That takes strength.
That takes self-awareness.
That takes restraint.

$$\bullet \quad \bullet \quad \bullet \quad \bullet \quad \bullet$$

How to Lead Without Ego

- Say "you're right" when someone else sees something you missed
- Take the harder shift
- Ask for upward feedback—and mean it
- Publicly praise your team's wins
- Say "I don't know" when you don't—and then go find the answer
- Make room for someone else to lead—even when you could do it faster

$$\bullet \quad \bullet \quad \bullet \quad \bullet \quad \bullet$$

When you lead without ego:
- Your team trusts you more
- They bring you issues faster
- They try harder, because they feel safe doing so
- They stay longer, because they don't feel stepped on

The store runs smoother.
And you spend less time performing—and more time **building.**

CHAPTER 11
How to Handle Being Wrong in Front of Your Team

Every leader makes mistakes.

Sometimes it's a wrong decision.
Sometimes it's something you said too quickly.
Sometimes it's calling someone out publicly when it should've been private.
Sometimes it's just... silence when your team needed more.

Whatever it is, it happens.

What matters most isn't perfection—it's **what you do next.**

•   •   •   •   •

There's no faster way to lose your team's trust than to pretend you're never wrong.
But there's also no faster way to earn their trust than to **own it when you are.**

That's what separates strong leaders from insecure ones.

•   •   •   •   •

I've gotten it wrong before.

I've jumped to conclusions about a situation before asking questions.
I've misread customer feedback and passed that pressure onto the team.
I've reacted with frustration when I should've taken a beat.

But every time I've owned it—directly, calmly, and quickly—something happened:

My team leaned in.

They didn't lose respect for me.

They respected me *more*—because I was willing to hold myself to the same standard I asked of them.

• • • • •

If you want your people to take accountability, they have to see **you** do it first.

That means saying things like:

- "I got that wrong."
- "I overreacted, and I want to walk it back."
- "I made a decision without hearing the full story—let's reset."
- "You were right to question that—I should've handled it differently."

These moments are uncomfortable. But they're powerful.

Because they say:

"I'm not here to be perfect. I'm here to grow—with you."

• • • • •

Why Leaders Avoid Admitting They're Wrong

- Fear of looking weak
- Belief that authority depends on certainty
- Insecurity from upper management pressure
- Habit—especially if they were never led by someone who admitted mistakes

But avoiding it doesn't make it go away.

It just teaches your team that:

- You won't listen
- You can't be trusted
- Mistakes are shameful—not fixable

That mindset kills growth faster than any metric.

· · · · ·

How to Handle It (Without Undermining Yourself)

1. **Own it clearly**
    Don't sugarcoat. Don't excuse. Just name it.

2. **Be timely**
    The longer you wait, the less genuine it feels.

3. **Keep it calm**
    No dramatic apologies—just grounded accountability.

4. **Close the loop**
    Let them know how you'll prevent it from happening again.

5. **Move forward**
    Don't dwell. Model accountability, then keep leading.

· · · · ·

You don't need to tear yourself down.
You just need to show that leadership means owning both the wins and the misses.

When you do that, you create a team that:
- Speaks up faster
- Trusts you deeper
- Feels safer making mistakes and learning from them
- Holds themselves to a higher standard—because *you do, too*

· · · · ·

Your team doesn't expect you to be flawless.
They expect you to be **fair. Real. Human.**

And when you show them what that looks like in leadership?

They'll show up with more grace, more honesty, and more commitment than you ever imagined.

PART II
Fixing the Floor

Now that we've exposed the leadership gaps,
this section shows how to fix them at ground level.

CHAPTER 12
Why Folding Tables Matter More Than You Think

You can learn everything you need to know about a store by how their folding tables look at 2:00 p.m.

Not at opening.
Not ten minutes before a visit.
But right in the middle of a regular, unfiltered shift.

Because folding tables don't lie.

They show you if there's ownership.
They show you if there's pace.
They show you if someone took the time to train—or just told people, *"Fix it when you can."*

• • • • •

A messy table in the middle of a rush? That happens.
But a messy table that stays messy two hours after a rush?
That tells you everything.

It tells you the team doesn't take pride.
Or maybe they don't know how to fold properly.
Or maybe they *do*—but they've been corrected so many times that they no longer care.

The table becomes a metaphor.
Not just for presentation—but for **standards**.

• • • • •

I've always said:

"Window displays are free retail."

And folding tables? They're the frontlines of that retail battlefield.

They're the first touchpoint for many customers.
They reflect your brand.
They reflect your team.
And most importantly—they reflect your leadership.

• • • • •

I've seen folding tables that looked like sculpture.
Perfect edges, consistent spacing, sharp color blocking.
Those stores were often some of the most organized, high-performing teams I worked with.

Because no one folds a table like that by accident.
It takes **training. Follow-up. Standards. Accountability.**

It takes leadership.

• • • • •

But I've also seen the opposite.

Tables that looked like laundry piles.
Shirts half-hung, sizes backwards, stock tags popping out like confetti.
And it wasn't because the team didn't care.

It was because **no one taught them why it mattered.**

They were told *"straighten the table"*—but never shown how.
Never told the why.
Never recognized when they got it right.

• • • • •

Here's what folding tables actually teach:

- Attention to detail
- Ownership
- Product handling
- Visual strategy
- And pacing—because you can't take 20 minutes to fold one stack

It's where rookies learn the rhythm of the store.
It's where veterans model standards for the next generation.
It's where leaders can quietly raise the bar *without saying a word*.

•　•　•　•　•

So no—it's not *just folding a shirt*.
It's teaching discipline.
It's reinforcing pride.
It's turning repetition into *precision*.

And if your tables are sloppy? Don't blame the team.

Start with the training.
Start with the follow-up.
Start with the standard you've allowed.

Because how your store folds clothes…
is often how your team *handles everything else*.

CHAPTER 13
Visual Merchandising: The Silent Salesperson

Every product on the sales floor is telling a story.

The question is—**who's writing it?**

Because if your visuals aren't strategic, they're random.
And if they're random, they're not selling.

Visual merchandising isn't decoration.
It isn't just about what "looks good."
It's about movement. Flow. Psychology. Storytelling.

It's the *silent salesperson*—working even when your staff is distracted.

•   •   •   •   •

I've worked with plenty of stores where visuals were an afterthought.

Tables thrown together.
Color stories that clashed.
Key pieces buried in the middle of racks.
Fixtures too tight to shop.
Dead zones created by poor lighting or clunky placement.

Then came the complaints:

"Why isn't this item selling?"
"We just marked all this down and no one touched it."
"We had great product, it just didn't move."

The problem wasn't the product.

It was the *presentation.*

· · · · ·

A strong visual setup answers these questions before a customer ever speaks:

- What's the story here?
- What's new?
- What's the best value?
- What should I feel when I see this?
- What do I want to touch first?

Done right, visual merchandising **leads the customer through the store—** from the front window to the fitting room and right to the register.

It makes them stop. Pick up. Try on. Ask.

That's *sales behavior.*
And visuals create it long before your best associate says a word.

· · · · ·

Here's what visual merchandising really is:

- **A floor plan that makes sense**
- **A fixture strategy that creates movement**
- **A color story that feels seasonal, balanced, and shoppable**
- **A balance between statement pieces and volume drivers**
- **A daily habit—not a quarterly panic**

And most importantly? It's **trainable.**

You don't need a visual degree.
You need awareness, intention, and a team that knows the "why."

· · · · ·

When I coach visuals, I don't just give layout notes.

I train the team to ask:

- "What's the first thing they see when they walk in?"
- "Would I stop and look at this table if I weren't working here?"
- "Is this helping the customer make a decision—or creating noise?"

If the answer is "I don't know," the layout isn't ready.

· · · · ·

Great visuals do three things:
1. Highlight what you want to sell
2. Build value in the customer's mind
3. Remove friction from the shopping experience

If your layout isn't doing that, it's not neutral—it's costing you.

· · · · ·

And here's the most overlooked truth:
Visuals are for your *team* just as much as they're for your customers.

Clear fixture logic = less restocking time.
Strong table standards = less confusion during resets.
Planned walls = less reliance on the manager to approve everything.

Visual merchandising creates **confidence**, not just conversion.

CHAPTER 14
Your Staff Isn't Lazy—They're Undertrained

"They're lazy."

It's one of the most common complaints I hear from retail managers and owners.

"They just stand around."
"They don't hustle."
"They never restock unless I tell them."
"They're always on their phones."
"They don't take initiative."

And sometimes? Sure. Someone's not pulling their weight.

But most of the time, it's not laziness.

It's undertraining.

• • • • •

You can't expect people to take initiative if you've only taught them to follow orders.
You can't expect independent thinking if you've micromanaged every task.
You can't expect consistency if you haven't built muscle memory.

And if all they ever hear is what they're doing wrong?

They're not going to try harder.
They're going to stop trying at all.

• • • • •

I've seen it happen in dozens of stores.

A new hire gets a rushed walkthrough.
They shadow someone who half-explains things.
They get one "training shift" and are then expected to perform at a level it took you years to master.

When they fall short, they're labeled.
Dismissed.
Talked about in the back room.
Written off as "not a retail person."

But you didn't give them a chance to become one.

$$\bullet \quad \bullet \quad \bullet \quad \bullet \quad \bullet$$

Here's the hard truth:
If your team doesn't know what great looks like, you can't expect them to deliver it.

Training isn't about showing someone once.
It's about building a rhythm.
It's about explaining the *why*, not just the *how*.
It's about checking in often—not to babysit, but to reinforce.

Because people don't grow from being thrown in.
They grow from being taught, coached, corrected, and supported—on repeat.

$$\bullet \quad \bullet \quad \bullet \quad \bullet \quad \bullet$$

Ask yourself:
- Have I set clear standards and reinforced them consistently?
- Have I trained them on pacing, not just process?
- Have I coached them through tough situations—or just expected them to know what to do?
- Have I built a team of thinkers—or a team of task-doers?

Because "lazy" behavior often looks like:

- Not knowing what to do next
- Not understanding the priority
- Not feeling ownership
- Not being coached on how to improve

•　•　•　•　•

The best store teams I've led weren't full of "naturals."
They were full of people who were given the **space and structure** to learn.

They were asked for their input.
They were coached regularly.
They were praised when they got it right.
And they were corrected with care—not with sarcasm or shame.

That's what builds initiative.
That's what builds trust.
That's what builds stores that run without needing constant supervision.

•　•　•　•　•

If you're frustrated with your team, start with training.

Not just what you covered in orientation.
Not just what you *think* they know.
But what they've been taught, reinforced, observed, and supported on.

Because 9 times out of 10?

Your staff isn't lazy.
They're undertrained.

CHAPTER 15
Clienteling Starts with Trust, Not Scripts

Clienteling is one of the most overused—and underdelivered—buzzwords in retail.

You hear it everywhere:

"We build relationships here."
"We pride ourselves on clienteling."
"We don't sell—we connect."

But in too many stores, it's just a fancy word taped to a bad habit:
- Pushing product under the guise of personalization
- Rushing into "add-ons" before earning the customer's trust
- Using the same five opening lines that every shopper has already heard three times that day

That's not clienteling.
That's pressure with a smile.

• • • • •

Real clienteling starts before the sale.
It starts with how you listen.
How you observe.
How you make the customer feel—**not how fast you mention the loyalty program.**

And like everything else in retail:
If your team isn't doing it well, it's probably because they haven't been shown what "great" looks like.

· · · · ·

Here's what clienteling is *not*:

- "Are you shopping for anything special today?"
- "We have a promotion going on right now."
- "Let me know if you need a size."
- "You can sign up at checkout for rewards."

That's generic. That's passive. That's forgettable.

· · · · ·

Here's what clienteling *is*:

- Reading body language and knowing when to engage
- Asking thoughtful, genuine questions
- Offering value before offering product
- Remembering a customer's past purchase—or how something fit last time
- Connecting over a detail they didn't expect you to notice

It's trust.
It's timing.
It's knowing that a sale built on rapport is more valuable than a quick upsell that leaves them feeling pushed.

· · · · ·

Some of the best sales I've ever made came from not selling.

Just *being present*.
Talking about travel.
Asking what they were shopping for before suggesting what they should buy.

And then—when they trusted me—I offered something they didn't know they needed.
That's clienteling.

And they came back—because they remembered how they were treated, not just what they bought.

• • • • •

If your team struggles with this, coach them on *reading the moment*, not just hitting KPIs.

- Ask them to recap the customer's reason for being in the store
- Practice open-ended questions in downtime
- Show them how to pivot based on the customer's energy—not a script

Teach them that **every customer deserves a different approach**—because no two shopping missions are the same.

• • • • •

If you train your team to build trust first, they'll never need to feel like they're "selling."

Because the product becomes a solution.
The store becomes a space.
And your people? They become **partners** in the experience—not pressure points.

• • • • •

3 Simple Clienteling Habits That Create Repeat Business

6. **Use their name once—then again before they leave.**
   Names create connection. If a customer introduces themselves or gives their name at checkout, repeat it naturally before they leave:

"Thanks again, Monica—let me know how those jeans fit!"
That moment of recognition sticks with people longer than any coupon.

7. **Make one personal connection before making a product suggestion.**
   Before you recommend anything, connect first.

"That blazer reminds me of something you'd see in a fall campaign. Are you shopping for something specific, or just in a good mood today?"

If the customer smiles or shares a detail—*then* you've earned the product pivot.

8. **Follow up with purpose.**
   If you get permission to reach out—**make it matter**.
   Don't send, "Just checking in."
   Instead, say:

"Hey, we just got a new drop that reminds me of what you were looking for last time. Want me to hold your size?"
That's personal. That's thoughtful. That's what keeps them coming back.

• • • • •

Clienteling isn't a policy. It's a mindset.

And when your team learns how to earn trust first, *the results will follow.*

CHAPTER 16
Training Is Not One and Done

Most stores train people like this:
- A rushed tour of the sales floor
- A few hours shadowing someone who's not great at explaining
- A list of policies they won't remember
- A "you'll pick it up as you go" speech

Then a few weeks later?

"They're just not catching on."
"They don't really have the pace."
"They're not taking initiative."

But it's not their initiative that failed.
It's your **training system.**

· · · · ·

Training isn't something you do at the start of the job.

It's something you **build into the job**—every week, every shift, every leader, every associate.

Because when training is treated as a one-time event, what you're really teaching is:
- "We don't expect you to grow."
- "Figure it out on your own."
- "There's no real standard—just survive."

That's not culture. That's chaos.

• • • • •

The best stores I've ever led didn't have the best people on day one.
They had the best systems for turning good people into **great contributors** over time.

That happened because we trained:
- In layers
- On purpose
- With structure
- And with **follow-up**

• • • • •

Here's what strong, ongoing training actually looks like:
- **New hire orientation** that covers core expectations (pace, visuals, cleanliness, service)
- **Week 2 check-ins** focused on confidence, not just policy compliance
- **Weekly coaching themes** (e.g., how to greet vs. how to upsell)
- Mid-shift role plays or reviews in 2-3 minute bursts
- **Monthly refreshers** on things people *think* they know—but could do better

It's not about overloading people with content.
It's about reinforcing habits until they become second nature.

• • • • •

Great training answers these questions clearly:
- What does "great" look like here?
- How do we correct mistakes—without creating fear?
- How will I know if I'm improving?
- How often will I be coached—and by who?

And if your current training program can't answer those?
You don't have a system. You have *guesswork*.

• • • • •

"You're not too busy to train—you're too disorganized to plan for it."

If you think you don't have time to train, I promise:
You're spending **way more time** correcting problems that proper training would've prevented in the first place.

• • • • •

The stores that thrive long-term don't just have talented people.
They have a rhythm for teaching, reinforcing, coaching, and correcting—with intention.

And that rhythm creates:
- Consistency
- Confidence
- Trust
- Lower turnover
- Higher engagement
- Better performance

• • • • •

Training isn't a task.
It's a system.
And once it's in place, your store doesn't just improve—it *stays* improved.

Because your people don't stop learning.
And neither do you.

CHAPTER 17
What Gets Scheduled Gets Done

Most struggling stores don't fail because people aren't working hard.

They fail because they're working hard on the wrong things—at the wrong times—with no structure in place.

Ask a team what they're supposed to be doing today and you'll get a dozen different answers:

- "We're catching up on shipment."
- "I think we're resetting clearance."
- "We were told to clean the back, but then something else came up."
- "Honestly? No idea."

That's not a lazy store.

That's a directionless one.

· · · · ·

In retail, time is your most limited resource—and your greatest tool.

You'll never have "enough time" to do everything.

But if you're intentional, you will have time to do the right things.

That's why scheduling matters. Not just for coverage—but for clarity.

What gets scheduled gets done.

What doesn't? Gets pushed. Delayed. Forgotten. Ignored.

And then? You fall behind.

Team morale drops.

Leadership looks disorganized.

Customers feel the ripple effect without even knowing why.

· · · · ·

I've worked in stores that ran purely off memory and reaction.

Managers juggling 15 priorities in their head, trying to adjust on the fly.

They were constantly busy—but rarely productive.

Shipment piled up.

Visual updates were always "coming soon."

Training got pushed.

Performance issues lingered.

And nothing ever felt finished.

Compare that to stores where there was a clear weekly rhythm:
- Mondays = shipment
- Tuesdays = replenishment and transfers
- Wednesdays = visual projects
- Thursdays = coaching and reviews
- Fridays = stock recovery
- Weekends = sales and support

It wasn't perfect—but it was predictable.

And in retail, predictability creates confidence.

· · · · ·

When your team knows the flow, they move with purpose.

When they don't, they spend half the day asking, guessing, or waiting.

And that's how time gets lost—not to laziness, but to lack of clarity.

• • • • •

What Poor Scheduling Really Costs

- Burnout: Team members feel like they're always behind, always reacting, and never "done." It's exhausting.
- Disorganization: Shipment sits too long. Projects never finish. Customers notice gaps in product and service.
- Inconsistent Standards: Tasks get rushed or skipped entirely. Every shift runs differently. Expectations blur.
- Leadership Distrust: Associates stop checking the plan—because there isn't one. Morale drops. Turnover rises.
- Missed Sales: Promo execution is late. Merchandising is sloppy. Customers don't see new product until it's old.

• • • • •

Here's what great leaders schedule:
- Shipment processing
- Visual flips and table resets
- Backstock audits and bin checks
- Floor walks with staff coaching
- Sales strategy sessions
- Follow-up on previous assignments
- Downtime tasks for slow shifts

It's not about micromanaging—it's about being proactive.

Because when you don't plan your time, someone else will waste it for you.

• • • • •

If your store feels chaotic, check your calendar.

Is it reactive?

Is it random?

Or is it intentional?

The difference between average and excellent isn't just talent or staffing.

It's rhythm.

It's follow-through.

It's structure.

Because in this business—what gets scheduled gets done.

If your team feels scattered, it's rarely about talent—it's about timing. And timing is something you control.

CHAPTER 18
The Backstock Is the Truth

If you want to know what kind of leader runs a store, don't look at the sales numbers.

Don't look at the front tables or the customer reviews.

Go straight to the backstock.

Because the back tells the truth.

• • • • •

The sales floor can be staged.

You can rush to clean it before a visit.

You can coach people to smile and greet.

You can move numbers around to make reports look better than they are.

But the back?

The backstock exposes everything you've neglected:
- Poor communication
- No follow-through
- Disorganized leadership
- Lack of systems
- No accountability
- No pride

• • • • •

I've walked into stores that looked immaculate out front—pristine, welcoming, high energy.

But once I stepped into the back room, it all fell apart.

Boxes unopened for weeks.

Returns stacked without tags.

Paper signs taped to shelves instead of a system.

Missing markdowns.

Merchandise stuffed wherever it fit.

And the person in charge? Still claiming they "run a tight ship."

You don't.

Because a store's backroom is a reflection of what leadership allows.

• • • • •

Here's the reality most people in corporate don't want to admit:

Operations are just as important as sales.

Yes, revenue matters.

Yes, visuals matter.

But if your backroom is a disaster, your team is in a constant state of distraction, frustration, and fatigue.

They can't find what they need.

They don't know what's coming in.

They're guessing on stock levels.

And they're spending their energy putting out fires instead of creating results.

That's not sustainable.

And over time, it becomes culture.

● ● ● ● ●

I've always believed: how you do the unseen parts of the job reveals who you are as a leader.

Do you:

- Teach a system—or just point and demand?
- Regularly check the back—or only when you're panicking before a visit?
- Make time to train your team on backstock routines—or expect them to "just figure it out"?
- Know where everything is—or have to ask every time?

You don't have to run a perfect stockroom.

But you do have to run an intentional one.

Because when your back is clean, labeled, and respected?

The team works faster.

Inventory is accurate.

Restocks happen before they're asked.

And customers feel it—even if they never see it.

● ● ● ● ●

What a Messy Backroom Actually Costs

- Labor: Hours wasted looking for items, repulling misstocked product, and backtracking on mistakes that could've been avoided with a system.
- Time: Delays in floor replenishment, missing out on sales because product isn't ready or visible.
- Shrink: Items misplaced, stolen, or damaged due to lack of control— especially during peak seasons.

- Morale: Associates disengage when they're constantly cleaning up leadership's mess instead of being set up to win.
- Training Cost: Without clear systems, every new hire gets a different version of "how to backstock," leading to inconsistency and higher error rates.

· · · · ·

The truth is, anyone can sell during a promo.

Anyone can straighten a table for a walkthrough.

But the backroom? That's where consistency lives.

That's where your systems either hold—or fall apart.

So if you want to know how strong your leadership is, don't look at the floor.

Look at the back.

Because the backstock is the truth.

CHAPTER 19
The Leader Who Takes the Bad Shift

Leadership doesn't show up in the morning meeting.
It shows up when the schedule drops.

Everyone sees it.
Everyone scrolls.
Everyone spots that late Friday close.
The solo Saturday opener.
The double shipment + floor flip Tuesday.

And everyone checks to see whose name is there.

If it's yours? That says something.
If it never is? That says something louder.

• • • • •

There's a different kind of trust that gets built when you take the worst shift on the board.
Not because you were forced to.
Not because you needed coverage.
But because that's who you are.

The leader who shows up when it's hard.
The leader who doesn't push the weight downhill.
The leader who says, "I've got this one."

• • • • •

I learned that lesson early in one of my first leadership roles.

It was the holidays, and I was new to making the schedule. I was still earning trust and trying to balance what was best for the store and best for the team.

We were prepping for New Year's Day, and I knew most of the team would be celebrating the night before. So I made the call to let everyone enjoy their NYE and sleep in. I scheduled myself and one other non-partier to open the next morning.

It wasn't about being a martyr. It was about doing right by the people I was leading.

What happened next surprised me.

Two staff members who weren't scheduled showed up anyway—just to help. They knew I was trying to support them, and they wanted to return the gesture. No one asked them to be there. They just showed up.

And it turned out to be a very busy morning.
We crushed it. Sales were strong. Energy was high. And most importantly—trust deepened.
They saw I was willing to take the weight, and they met me there.

That moment stuck with me.
It wasn't just a great sales day—it was the beginning of a leadership style built on shared ownership, mutual respect, and showing up for each other when it counts.

•   •   •   •   •

You don't always have to take the bad shift.
But you need to take it enough that no one questions whether you're willing to.

Because your team is watching.

And when they see you:
- Take the solo freight shift

- Stay late after a rough day
- Fill the holes when someone calls out
- Step in without making it a performance...

They remember.

And one day, they'll step in too—not because they have to, but because *they've seen it done right.*

· · · · ·

What Taking the Bad Shift Teaches

- You're not above it
- You practice what you preach
- You protect your team from burnout—not just talk about it
- You see the hard stuff and don't hand it off—you walk through it first

It's not about being everywhere.
It's about being **where it matters**, when it matters.

· · · · ·

Leadership isn't about building the perfect schedule for yourself.
It's about knowing when to take the weight so someone else can breathe.

And when you do that?

They'll go further for you.
They'll step in when you're tired.
They'll remember the way you showed up when no one expected it.

Because taking the bad shift isn't about time—it's about trust.

PART III
Building a Team That Works Without You

This section moves beyond fixing—
into delegation, coaching, and leadership development.

CHAPTER 20
The Manager's Real Job: Build Other Managers

If your store falls apart the moment you leave, you're not leading.

You're babysitting.

Great managers don't just build great results—they build **great people.**
People who can run things when you're off.
People who make decisions without constant input.
People who one day won't need your leadership—because they *grew up under it.*

· · · · ·

That's the real job.
Not just managing tasks.
Not just coaching performance.
But **developing future leaders** while you lead.

· · · · ·

Too often in retail, we gatekeep leadership.

Managers want to feel irreplaceable, so they hoard knowledge.
They don't delegate.
They overcorrect.
They make every decision—then wonder why their team is passive, hesitant, or uninvolved.

But here's the truth:

If your team can only function when you're there, that's not job security. That's leadership failure.

• • • • •

The best stores I've ever led didn't need me every second.
Because I built people who thought like leaders—even before they had the title.

I taught them to:
- Ask good questions
- Understand the *why* behind every standard
- Own outcomes—not just tasks
- Train others with care and clarity
- Speak up when something felt off

And when they messed up, I didn't punish. I coached.

Small mistakes while growing? That's called **progress.**

• • • • •

Signs Someone *Is* Ready to Lead:
- They take pride in their work—especially the parts no one sees
- They train others with consistency, not shortcuts
- They're calm in chaos, and steady under pressure
- They take initiative without needing credit
- They care about the store even when they're not on the clock

If you see this—*lean in.*
Give them stretch opportunities. Shadow time. Ask their opinion.
Start calling them up to more—even before it's official.

• • • • •

Signs Someone Is *Not Yet* Ready to Lead:
- They only step up when asked—and disappear when no one's looking

- They complain about being "in charge," but avoid accountability
- They want the title, but not the work
- They correct others harshly or inconsistently
- They create cliques or drama, not connection
- They struggle with feedback—or take it personally

These aren't disqualifiers. They're **development points.**
You don't have to say "no forever." Just:

"Not yet—and here's what I want to work on with you."

• • • • •

The goal isn't just to promote someone.
It's to **prepare them** so when they get promoted, they don't just survive—
they lead.

And the more people you grow into leaders?
The less *you* have to carry every shift, every decision, every fire drill.

That's how your job becomes sustainable.
Enjoyable.
And respected.

• • • • •

Because your job isn't to stay at the top.
It's to **pull people up behind you.**

And when you do?

You don't just build a team.
You build a culture that sustains itself—**with or without you.**

CHAPTER 21
Servant Leadership on the Sales Floor

Servant leadership is the heart of this book.

It's not a gimmick.
It's not trendy.
And it's not for people trying to "get ahead" by doing less.

It's for the leaders who want to build teams that don't just work—but work with purpose, with pride, and with each other.

Servant leadership isn't about being passive. It's not just being "nice."
It's about stepping up with humility, removing friction, and showing your team—through action—that you're with them, not above them.

• • • • •

One of my core principles has always been:

"I will never ask an employee to do something they haven't seen me do two or three times before."

That's not just about fairness. It's about **credibility**.

If you've seen your leader:

- Clean the bathrooms
- Fold denim until their fingertips hurt
- Vacuum the floors
- Space out product during a last-minute flip
- Take out the trash at closing...

...then when they ask *you* to do it? You don't roll your eyes. You do it—because they've done it, too.

They've modeled the expectation.
They've led with example, not entitlement.
And that's what servant leadership *looks like*.

· · · · ·

"Work for Your People"

I've had days where I was dead tired. Where I could've "led from the back." But the moment the rush hit, I clocked back in.

Not because I had to. But because that's the job.

When your staff sees you hit the sales floor—not just to "check on things," but to hustle alongside them—they feel something shift. They *match* your energy. They respect your pace. They trust your lead.

"Work for your people, and they'll work harder for you."

And it's true.

If your team believes you're willing to do whatever it takes to make the shift work—they'll go further than they ever would out of obligation.

· · · · ·

The Misconception About Servant Leadership

Some managers hear "servant leadership" and think it means giving up authority.

That's wrong.

Servant leadership isn't soft.
It's **structured. Present. Grounded. Firm.**

You hold high standards—but you help people reach them.

You give clear direction—but stay accessible.
You give trust—but remain involved.

As Tony Bridwell puts it:

"Your influence with others increases when you lead with love instead of judgment."

Love in leadership isn't weakness.
It's listening. It's investing. It's giving someone your presence when it would be easier to give them orders.

• • • • •

Leading by Example (Without Burning Out)

Being a servant leader doesn't mean you do everything.
It means you show the *path*—and walk it first.

You fold the wall before teaching how to do it faster.
You explain the why behind policies instead of saying "just because."
You train your key holder how to lead a floor walk by *inviting them into one.*

And then you let go—slowly—so they grow.

You don't micromanage.
But you don't disappear, either.

• • • • •

5 Questions to Check If You're Leading with Service

1. Have they seen me do this task well—more than once?
2. Do I explain the *why*, or just give instructions?
3. Do I work the hard shifts—or only the light ones?
4. When's the last time I coached in the moment—without judgment?
5. Do they believe I'd go through the fire with them—or just send orders from the office?

· · · · ·

Real Examples of Servant Leadership in Retail

- The leader who vacuums the floor with the openers, not just points at the checklist
- The manager who folds side by side with a struggling new hire—not just redoes it later
- The owner who rolls racks to the fitting room during a 30-minute lunch rush without making a show of it
- The leader who quietly throws away trash, resets shoes, or zips jackets— even after a 10-hour shift

These moments matter more than you think.

They don't just keep the store clean.
They build **trust**.
And trust builds **culture**.

· · · · ·

Servant Leadership Is the Long Game

You don't always see immediate results.
You might get questioned. Some people won't understand.
They'll say, "You're doing too much," or "Don't you have more important things to do?"

Ignore that.

Because six months from now?
Your team won't just be performing—they'll be leading.

They'll hold the standard when you're off.
They'll coach the new hire without being told.
They'll take care of the store—not out of fear—but out of pride.

That's servant leadership.

It multiplies your presence.
It outlasts your schedule.
It cements your impact.

• • • • •

You don't need to have the loudest voice in the room.
You just need to show up, step in, and serve well.

If you do?

You won't have to chase respect.

You'll earn it—*quietly, consistently, and completely.*

CHAPTER 22
You Don't Need to Be Feared to Be Respected

There's still a dangerous idea floating around retail management:

"If they don't fear you, they won't listen."

That mindset doesn't lead—it intimidates.
It doesn't develop—it damages.
And it doesn't earn respect—it demands compliance.

Respect built on fear isn't respect at all. It's survival.

• • • • •

I've worked under that kind of leadership.

The kind that raises their voice just to make a point.
The kind that confuses intensity with influence.
The kind that makes people perform—*but only while they're watching.*

Because once that boss walks away, the motivation walks with them.

Why?
Because no one trusts a leader who rules with fear.

• • • • •

You don't need fear to lead effectively.
You need consistency.
You need fairness.
You need courage.

And you need standards you're willing to model and defend—with calm confidence.

When your team respects your presence, your example, and your follow-through—*that's real leadership.*

•　•　•　•　•

Here's the difference:

Fear-based leadership leads to:

- Avoidance
- Silence
- Resentment
- High turnover
- Burnout
- Compliance without commitment

Respect-based leadership leads to:

- Ownership
- Honest feedback
- Loyalty
- Growth
- Team stability
- Performance that lasts when you're not there

•　•　•　•　•

A team that respects you will:

- Ask questions because they want to improve
- Push themselves because they care—not because they're scared
- Step up for others because that's what you've modeled

A team that fears you will:

- Withhold mistakes

- Tell you what you want to hear
- Smile while they write their two weeks' notice

. . . . .

The most powerful leaders I've known were the calmest in chaos.
They didn't explode when things went wrong—they asked the right questions.
They didn't tear people down—they taught them how to rise.

And the team followed them—not out of fear, but because they *believed in them.*

. . . . .

If you've led with fear before, it doesn't mean you're broken.
It means you were taught wrong.
Retail often rewards volume over voice, speed over strategy, authority over connection.

But that's not sustainable.

Real respect comes when your team knows:
- You have their back
- You tell the truth
- You lead with strength *and* stability
- You care about more than just the numbers

. . . . .

Don't chase fear.
Don't mistake obedience for respect.
And don't confuse intimidation with influence.

Respect is earned—not enforced.

And when you lead with integrity, consistency, and trust?

You don't need to be feared.

You'll be followed—because your team chooses to.

CHAPTER 23
How to Create a Culture of Ownership

If you've ever had to remind someone five times to fix the same table, this chapter is for you.

If you've ever come back from a day off to find shipment untouched, the floor reset incorrectly, or customers complaining about things that should've been basic—that's not just a performance issue.

That's a culture issue.

And more specifically, it's a **lack of ownership.**

•　•　•　•　•

Ownership isn't a personality trait.
It's not reserved for your "strongest" employees.
It's not something people just bring with them when they're hired.

It's taught. Modeled. Reinforced. Expected.

And it shows up everywhere:
- In how someone reacts when something goes wrong
- In whether they restock without being told
- In how they handle the floor when you're not there
- In whether they take pride in the job—or just complete it

•　•　•　•　•

A culture of ownership means your team *cares* about the outcome—because they see themselves as part of it.

They don't say, "That's not my job."
They don't wait for permission to solve obvious problems.
They don't look the other way when something's wrong.

They act.
Because they've been empowered to, and they've seen what that looks like in action.

· · · · ·

What Teaches Ownership?

1. **Clarity of expectations**
   You can't own a standard you don't understand.

2. **Visible leadership**
   When your team sees *you* take ownership, they're more likely to mimic that behavior.

3. **Trust and autonomy**
   When you trust your team to run something without micromanaging, they step into responsibility.

4. **Follow-up, not just follow-through**
   People need to know that ownership is noticed, appreciated, and expected again tomorrow—not just once.

5. **Conversations, not corrections**
   "How would you have handled that differently?" builds more ownership than "Don't let that happen again."

· · · · ·

I've seen the difference between stores that *talk* ownership and stores that *live* it.

One store has a team where:
- Every associate knows their zone and checks it constantly

- Team members hold each other to standards
- The manager can step away—and the momentum doesn't stop
- Results are consistent—even during turnover

Another store has:
- A leadership team constantly cleaning up *after* their staff
- Associates who wait to be told what to do
- The same issues popping up week after week
- Good people burning out because they're carrying the weight alone

Important note:

Cleaning up after someone is *not* the same as modeling servant leadership.

As a servant leader, you show the way, shoulder the load with your team, and coach in real time.

But when you clean up everyone's slack—*instead of holding people accountable*—you're not serving. You're enabling.

· · · · ·

What Kills Ownership?

1. **Overcorrecting**

   When leaders jump in to fix everything themselves, they teach the team not to bother.

2. **Micromanagement**

   When you give no room for ownership, you get no behavior that reflects it.

3. **Favoritism**

   If expectations shift depending on who's working, people check out.

4. **Inconsistency**

   When the standard changes by the day, no one knows what to own.

5. **Lack of follow-up**
   If no one checks the task, no one owns the result.

6. **No praise, only correction**
   When effort is invisible, it disappears.

· · · · ·

If your store is stuck in a reactive loop—constantly playing cleanup, correcting the same things, and carrying the same frustrations—you don't need new people.

You need **a new standard for ownership.**

Start small:

- Assign table leadership by day.
- Rotate a daily "floor captain."
- Create pride around tasks.
- Build a habit of peer-to-peer accountability.

When your team starts to take pride in *something*, they'll eventually take pride in *everything.*

· · · · ·

Ownership doesn't mean perfection.
It means presence.
It means trying before asking.
It means following through—and knowing someone else depends on it.

The best part?

Ownership spreads faster than rules.
When even one or two people truly start to own the store with you, others notice.
They want to be part of that energy.

And eventually?

You stop reminding.

You stop babysitting.

And you start leading a team that leads itself.

CHAPTER 24
Coaching vs. Correcting: Know the Difference

Correction is easy.

Correction is:
- "Fix this."
- "Don't do that again."
- "That's not how we do it."

It's quick. It's direct. And sometimes, it's necessary.

But if correction is the only leadership tool you use?
You're not building anyone—you're just managing mistakes.

That's why you need **coaching.**

• • • • •

Coaching is harder—but it's where real growth happens.

Correction stops a behavior.
Coaching changes a mindset.

Correction fixes the table.
Coaching develops the associate who will fix it right without being told.

• • • • •

The Big Difference

Correction is about the task.
Coaching is about the person.

Correction says: "You did that wrong."
Coaching says: "Let's look at what happened and how to get better."

Correction points out the mistake.
Coaching teaches how to handle the situation better next time.

· · · · ·

If your team fears feedback, it's probably because they've only been corrected.

When people feel constantly "called out" instead of built up, they stop asking for help. They get defensive. They retreat.
And they repeat the same issues, because no one ever helped them understand the *why*.

· · · · ·

Let me be clear: There's nothing wrong with correction when it's used properly.
But it should never be your **default**.

Your role as a leader isn't just to enforce standards—it's to help people *reach* them.

· · · · ·

When to Correct

- Safety violations
- Repeated behaviors already coached
- Policy breaches
- Disrespect or behavior that compromises the team

Correction in these cases should be:
- Direct
- Private
- Calm

- Solution-oriented

And it should always be followed by a reset:

"Let's make sure this doesn't happen again. What do you need from me to help support that?"

• • • • •

When to Coach

- First-time mistakes
- Confidence issues
- Slow progress from someone trying to improve
- Missed opportunities in sales, visuals, or customer service
- Anything where the person would benefit from explanation—not just critique

Coaching sounds like:
- "Walk me through what you were thinking during that interaction."
- "What do you think went well there—and what could have gone better?"
- "Let's try that again together and break it down."
- "What would you try differently next time?"

That approach doesn't just change behavior.
It **teaches self-awareness**—which builds better teammates *and* future leaders.

• • • • •

One of my favorite things to see is an employee coaching another.

Not correcting. Coaching.

It means the culture is spreading.
It means they're not just following orders—they understand what "great" looks like and how to help others reach it.

You don't get that through constant critique.
You get it through coaching that creates confidence.

•　•　•　•　•

A team that's corrected will do the job.
A team that's coached will *own it*.

Because they're not working out of fear.
They're working with clarity.

CHAPTER 25
Mentoring Employees Who Might Outgrow You

Let's get one thing out of the way:

If someone leaves your store because they've grown into something bigger, that's not a loss.
That's a win.

It means you did your job.
You built someone up.
You developed confidence, skill, and ownership—enough for them to step into a larger opportunity.

"Real leaders create space for others to grow—even if that growth takes them somewhere else."
—Tony Bridwell

And if you're doing this right? It won't just happen once.
It'll happen often.

• • • • •

The goal of great leadership isn't to build a team that *needs* you.
It's to build people who can eventually lead others—even if it's not under your roof.

That's the difference between **managing for performance** and **mentoring for potential.**

• • • • •

In retail, it's easy to hold people too tightly.

You find a rockstar.

They make your job easier.

They anticipate what you need.

They build trust with the team.

They train new hires like pros.

And suddenly you start thinking, *"I can't lose them."*

But the moment that mindset kicks in, you stop growing them.

You stop challenging them.

You start protecting your comfort—and holding back theirs.

That's how resentment grows.

• • • • •

I've mentored people who left me and took leadership roles I once hoped they'd fill on my team.

One of the most meaningful examples came from someone I'll refer to here as ASM C.

They left the company years ago—but what happened afterward is what mattered.

One day, long after they'd moved on, they reached out to share a personal milestone.

They told me where they were working. What they'd accomplished. And—unprompted—they thanked me.

They told me I had been the most impactful manager they'd worked for.

That I'd given them the tools, the confidence, and the coaching that stuck with them.

That's the goal.

Not to hold on—but to send them forward *better*.

• • • • •

Here's how to mentor someone who might outgrow you:

- **Let go of ownership—but not accountability.**
  Give them space to lead, while still holding them to the standard.

- **Speak to their future, not just their task list.**
  Ask what they want next—and start preparing them for it.

- **Give them real leadership moments.**
  Let them run floor walks. Debriefs. Training sessions. Give feedback and coach them after.

- **Normalize growth.**
  Talk openly about next steps. Don't make them feel guilty for wanting more.

- **Build a bench.**
  Always be developing multiple team members—not just one "golden child."

"It's not leadership if it ends with you."
—Vic Keller

•　•　•　•　•

The truth is, people are going to leave eventually.

The question is:
Will they leave because they're burnt out—or because they were built up?

Only one of those is a legacy you can be proud of.

•　•　•　•　•

When someone says,

"Everything I know about leadership started with you,"

That matters more than a sales goal.
More than a clean audit.

More than a single year's retention.

Because when you build someone to outgrow the store—you build something that actually lasts.

CHAPTER 26

Holding the Line Without Burning Bridges

Leadership isn't just about setting the standard.
It's about protecting it—*without damaging the people you're trying to build up.*

That's the line.

You can't run a successful store by being everyone's best friend.
But you also can't build a team worth keeping if you steamroll them every time they fall short.

The skill is in the middle:
Firm, not harsh.
Clear, not cold.
Supportive, not soft.

• • • • •

I've seen leaders lose good people because they couldn't deliver hard feedback without shaming.
I've seen others get walked over because they were too afraid to say no.

Neither one works.

You have to hold the line.
On cleanliness. On effort. On culture. On showing up. On tone. On follow-through.

Because if you don't?

- Your best employees leave
- Your standards collapse

- And your authority starts to erode—slowly, then all at once

But here's the key:

You don't have to burn a bridge to build accountability.

• • • • •

What "Holding the Line" Actually Looks Like

- Giving feedback directly, but with respect
- Repeating expectations without rolling your eyes
- Correcting in private
- Refusing to make exceptions that break trust
- Following up when a correction has already been given
- Staying consistent—even when someone pushes back

And when necessary?

- Writing someone up professionally—without personal jabs
- Saying "This isn't working anymore" with clarity, not cruelty
- Ending employment in a way that still gives someone dignity

• • • • •

Accountability without humanity is control.
But humanity without accountability is chaos.

Leadership means carrying both.

• • • • •

"If you bend every time someone pushes, they'll stop believing in the line at all."

Holding the line means honoring your word.
If you say being late matters—then it has to matter when it happens.
If you say visuals matter—then the wall can't sit broken for a week.

If you say respect is the culture—then gossip and sarcasm don't get a pass just because someone is high-performing.

• • • • •

Real Example: Correcting Without Damaging

One of the clearest memories I have of this came with someone I've mentioned before—ASM C.

They had one of the best attitudes and strongest customer service instincts I'd ever seen.
We had a small team. A new store. A lot of moving parts. And ASM C was quickly becoming the kind of assistant manager I could rely on to help build something strong.

But early on, we had a moment.

There was a customer issue—nothing major at first. But ASM C refused to help "my" customer. It felt like a line had been crossed. A little insubordination. A refusal to support when support was needed.

And I could've snapped.

I could've written him up. Called it defiance. Sent a message.

But something told me to pause.

So I waited until the next day. We sat down privately—off the floor, away from the cameras. I asked what was really going on.

And it came out: he was going through some personal issues at home.
Stress had spilled into the store, and he'd responded poorly—not because he didn't care, but because he was overwhelmed.

He didn't need punishment.
He needed perspective—and support.

So we talked. I coached. We worked through it together.

And from that moment on, we grew stronger. He stepped up. We led better—together.

And years later, we still talk. Still have mutual respect.

Because when you correct someone with clarity *and* care, they don't pull away.

They grow from it.

And that's how you hold the line—without burning the bridge.

• • • • •

How to Set Boundaries Without Breaking Relationships

1. **Start with clarity**

   People can't meet a standard that's vague or assumed.

2. **Assume good intent—but hold the outcome**

   You can acknowledge effort and still correct what didn't meet the mark.

3. **Coach in the moment**

   Don't bottle it up or wait until it's a bigger deal.

4. **Use calm tone, confident words**

   It's not about volume—it's about certainty.

5. **Follow through**

   One missed follow-up undoes five great conversations.

• • • • •

If someone disrespects your line, they're not being bold.
They're being taught that your standard is optional.

And every time that happens, the rest of your team watches.

They see if you meant what you said.
They see if it applies to everyone or just a few.

They see if you're strong enough to keep the promise *without losing the connection.*

That's what makes a leader durable—not just likable.

CHAPTER 27
The Wrong Hire Can Undo It All

You can spend years building a great team, a great rhythm, a great store.

But all it takes is one wrong hire—especially one left unchecked—to unravel everything.

I've seen it.

I've lived it.

And it's one of the hardest truths in retail:

You don't just hire skills. You hire culture.

• • • • •

The wrong person doesn't always come in as a manager.

Sometimes, they're a part-time hire who gets too comfortable.

Sometimes, they're someone promoted too soon—who lets a little title give them a false sense of authority.

Sometimes, they're just allowed to linger far too long, until their presence spreads like a slow, choking fog through the store.

• • • • •

At my own store—one I led for seven years—a toxic part-timer was hired and eventually moved up to full-time. That shift gave them power they never earned. They weren't coaching or leading. They were dividing.

Multiple coworkers came to me asking not to work on the same shift.

Others requested different days entirely.

And I said it then, and I stand by it now:

"If every single other employee has had an issue with this one new employee, and several have requested not to work on the same days or shifts as them, then that new hire is the problem—not the other employees."

But leadership wouldn't listen.

And worse—they hired another just like them.

Soon, my high-functioning store became something else.

A place where gossip ruled, where demeaning comments went unchecked, and where two toxic hires had more influence than the people who built it.

So I left.

Not because I wanted to.

But because leadership chose to protect dysfunction over culture.

• • • • •

It wasn't the first time.

In another role, I worked under the best boss I ever had.

But after they left, the new hire changed everything.

Within weeks, it became clear: this was someone who didn't respect the work that had been built.

And once again, I had to walk away from something I loved.

• • • • •

You can't build a healthy store culture while protecting toxic hires.

You can't retain talent if the wrong person is eroding it day by day.

And you can't fix a bad fit by ignoring the damage.

Because the longer you stay quiet, the more people you lose.

To burnout.

To resentment.

To better-run stores.

•   •   •   •   •

The wrong hire doesn't just underperform. They unbuild.

- They make good people want to leave
- They turn small frustrations into big problems
- They shift the team's focus from growth to defense
- They wear your high performers down until they check out—or quit

If that sounds familiar, you're not overreacting.

You're seeing clearly.

•   •   •   •   •

Warning Signs You've Hired the Wrong Person

- Team morale drops within days
- Associates begin avoiding or requesting shift changes
- Quiet employees disengage
- They "tattle" or twist quotes out of context to gain favor
- Conflict increases, often centered around one person
- High performers stop volunteering or going the extra mile
- Their presence shifts your energy as a leader—and not in a good way
- They demand loyalty instead of earning respect

•   •   •   •   •

The Cost of Keeping the Wrong Hire

- Lost Talent: Your best employees will leave first—because they know their worth
- Training Drain: Every departure costs you weeks of training and shadowing
- Culture Damage: One tolerated toxic personality can undo years of hard work
- Time Waste: You spend more time managing tension than building the team
- Customer Fallout: Turnover and tension affect service, even if customers can't name it
- Personal Burnout: Leaders who care eventually burn out from defending something no one else is protecting

• • • • •

You can't always prevent a wrong hire.

But you can prevent the fallout—if you act fast.

Leadership means protecting the culture.

Even if it's uncomfortable.

Even if you're "going against" someone you hired.

Because if you don't?

You won't just lose a good employee.

You'll lose your store's identity.

PART IV
The Self-Aware Leader

Here, we turn inward. These chapters cover habits, structure, and emotional maturity.

CHAPTER 28
You're Not Too Busy—You're Disorganized

If you've ever opened, closed, unpacked freight, fixed visuals, answered emails, and coached a new hire all in the same 10-hour shift—this isn't about effort.

This is about rhythm.

Because most retail leaders aren't lazy. They aren't avoiding responsibility. They're buried in it.

They're reacting instead of leading.
They're moving constantly—but not always moving forward.

So if everything feels chaotic all the time?
You're not failing.
You're just out of rhythm—and you can fix that faster than you think.

• • • • •

This chapter isn't a callout. It's a reset.

You don't need more hours. You need less noise.

Because the best leaders I've worked with? They're just as busy as anyone else. But they're organized.

They build structure where others let chaos take over.
And they make time for what matters—because they've made space to do it.

• • • • •

What Disorganization Feels Like

- A task list that only exists in your head
- Five half-finished jobs between 9 and noon
- Repeating the same directions three times a week
- Shipment sitting because no one knew it was coming
- Spending 30 minutes fixing a table you didn't train someone else to do right
- Rebuilding your day around one no-call, no-show—again

Sound familiar?

You're not broken. You're just carrying more than your systems can support.

• • • • •

The Truth About Time

Being "too busy" becomes an excuse.
Not intentionally—but quietly.

The longer you tell yourself, *"I don't have time to coach today,"* the more days pass without development.
The longer you say, *"We'll clean it up tomorrow,"* the mess becomes the norm.
The more tasks you push to the next day, the more you're running in circles.

That's how stores fall behind—not from lack of effort, but from lack of rhythm.

• • • • •

Busy vs. Effective

Busy leaders:

- Look overwhelmed
- Handle every fire themselves
- Chase issues instead of anticipating them

- Work all day, but finish nothing fully
- Say "yes" to everything, and then resent it

Effective leaders:
- Write it down
- Block time for coaching, prep, and planning
- Let go of perfection when progress will do
- Train their team to help carry the weight
- Focus on the three things that matter most

One looks chaotic.

The other looks *calm under pressure.*

That's the difference.

• • • • •

How to Reclaim the Rhythm

1. **Write it down**
   Get it out of your head. Mental checklists create stress and forgetfulness.

2. **Prioritize clearly**
   Everything is not urgent. Know what's essential vs. what's noise.

3. **Block your time**
   Don't just "plan to get to it." Schedule it. Protect it. Lead it.

4. **Use slow hours intentionally**
   Restock. Train. Audit. Don't waste lulls—they're your leverage.

5. **Train people to share the load**
   If you're too busy to train, you'll always be too busy to lead.

6. **Say no when you need to**
   Protect your time the same way you protect your team.

• • • • •

A Quick Self-Check

- Are you constantly behind—but not sure why?
- Are you working harder than ever but seeing less improvement?
- Do small issues feel heavier than they should?
- Are you putting off feedback, training, or follow-up?

If so, you're not lazy.

You're not distracted.

You're just overwhelmed by tasks you haven't structured yet.

And once you fix that?

You'll feel your leadership click back into place.

•   •   •   •   •

You don't need to "work more."

You need to **work with intention**.

Because structure doesn't restrict you—it *frees* you.

It gives you time to coach.

To breathe.

To be on the floor with your team instead of hiding behind a checklist you can't finish.

You don't need to hustle harder.

You need to lead smarter.

And it starts by getting out of the chaos you've learned to survive—and into the rhythm that lets you thrive.

CHAPTER 29
You Can't Be a Great Leader
If You're Running on Empty

You can't pour into others if you're completely drained.
You can't lead with patience, presence, or clarity if you haven't had a real break in weeks.
You can't build people if you're just surviving.

And yet—that's how too many retail leaders operate every single day.

Running on empty.
Running on adrenaline.
Running on guilt, pressure, panic, or caffeine.

· · · · ·

This chapter isn't about work-life balance in the corporate sense.
It's about the reality of leading a store—where the "life" part often gets pushed until after floor sets, after audits, after last-minute coverage, after everything else.

But if you don't make room to recharge, *you don't get to keep leading well.*

Because burnout doesn't usually show up as a breakdown.

It shows up as:
- Shorter fuse
- Passive coaching
- Avoiding tough conversations
- Feeling stuck but doing nothing about it

- Going numb to the wins
- Losing empathy for the team
- Dreading the schedule—no matter who's on it

Sound familiar?

You're not alone.
And you're not weak for needing a reset.

• • • • •

Why Leaders Ignore Their Own Burnout

- They confuse exhaustion with work ethic
- They feel guilty asking for time off
- They think "being there" all the time proves loyalty
- They believe that stepping back equals letting the team down
- No one modeled sustainable leadership for them—only survival

But here's the truth:

You can't be strong for your team if you're silently breaking down.

• • • • •

I've had to learn this the hard way.
You can care deeply. Show up. Serve. Support.
But if you never rest, you will start *resenting* the job you once loved.

That's when mistakes happen.
That's when coaching stops.
That's when leadership fades into auto-pilot.

And the team feels it—even if they don't know how to name it.

• • • • •

Signs You're Leading on Empty

- You feel guilty leaving on time
- You haven't had a lunch break in a week
- You're waking up dreading the shift—even when nothing's "wrong"
- You're constantly irritable with your strongest employees
- You're doing the tasks just to get through—not to build anything

If you see yourself here, it's not failure.
It's a signal.

And ignoring it won't make it go away—it'll just make it worse.

• • • • •

How to Refill the Tank

- **Take your breaks, fully**
  Not at the desk. Not while checking payroll. Actually leave the floor.

- **Schedule recharge time like a meeting**
  A walk. A day off. A slow morning. Protect it.

- **Let your team carry things, sometimes**
  They don't need you in every moment—give them space to step up.

- **Talk about it**
  Tell a peer. A mentor. Your leader. You're not less valuable because you're tired.

- **Remember the mission**
  Reflect on your *why*. What kind of leader do you want to be? How do you want to feel while doing it?

• • • • •

You don't earn extra points for burnout.
You don't gain credibility by running yourself into the ground.

You don't inspire your team by suffering silently.

You inspire them by showing what healthy, sustainable leadership looks like.

By stepping away when needed.
By protecting your energy *so you can give it back with intention.*
By staying human, not superhuman.

• • • • •

You can't lead well forever if you're running on fumes today.

So take care of the person behind the role.

Your team needs that version of you—*the full one.*
Not the one who's barely getting by.

PART V
Scaling & Legacy

You've led the store—
now lead it into the future.

CHAPTER 30
The Exit Plan – Leading So You Can Step Away

Most retail leaders don't think about the end of their role until it's already happening.

A promotion.
A transfer.
A life change.
Burnout.
Or worse—being replaced before you're ready.

But the best leaders don't wait for the exit to show up.
They plan for it—*on day one.*

Why?

Because the sign of great leadership isn't what happens when you're there.
It's what keeps happening *after you're gone.*

· · · · ·

This chapter isn't about quitting.
It's about building something that lasts beyond you.

Your systems.
Your culture.
Your team's ability to thrive without constant oversight.

Because when you build that?

You create a store that doesn't need rescuing every time the manager rotates out.

· · · · ·

What It Looks Like to Lead with an Exit Plan

- You train every employee like they'll one day run the floor
- You organize your notes, documents, and resources so they're accessible to others
- You delegate—not to get rid of tasks, but to build decision-making muscles
- You develop a "next up" mindset across your team
- You normalize growth and exits—so they're not traumatic, they're *expected*

Think of it like legacy-mode management:
You're still here. Still leading.
But you're always making sure the store can outlast your schedule.

That's not just smart.
It's **responsible**.

· · · · ·

I've taken over stores that were built on sand.

Nothing was written down.
No one knew how to run payroll.
The top performer was also the biggest morale killer, but no one had coached them.
The team was lost the moment the manager wasn't in the room.

And I've also walked into stores that practically ran themselves.
Because the person before me wasn't just a leader—they were a builder.

They left behind systems, trust, delegation, and people who were *ready*.

That should be the goal.

· · · · ·

"You don't build a team that depends on you. You build a team that reflects you—even after you're gone."

• • • • •

How to Build Toward Your Exit (Even If It's Not Soon)

1. **Build your bench now**
   Don't wait until you're tapped on the shoulder. Develop backups early.

2. **Document your standards and systems**
   If someone had to run the store tomorrow without you, could they?

3. **Give away pieces of your role slowly**
   Let others lead floor walks. Write schedules. Run huddles.

4. **Check for knowledge gaps**
   Don't assume they know it because they've seen it. Ask. Train again.

5. **Remove yourself from the center**
   Great stores aren't manager-led. They're team-run.

• • • • •

Here's the best part: when you lead like this, **you get your life back.**

You can take a vacation and not come home to chaos.
You can take a lunch break without twenty texts.
You can focus on development instead of putting out fires.

Because your team owns the day-to-day.
And that gives you the freedom to lead the big picture.

• • • • •

Don't wait to build your exit plan until it's forced on you.
Build it now—so that when the opportunity comes, *you're ready.*

And the store you leave behind?

It won't just survive.

It'll reflect the kind of leader you were all along.

CHAPTER 31
Leaving It Better Than You Found It

This is what it's all been building toward.

Not just better numbers.
Not just stronger coaching.
Not just cleaner floors or sharper visuals or more consistent operations.

But **impact**.

Leadership that lasts.
Culture that outlives you.
A team that stands taller because *you showed up differently*.

• • • • •

The retail world doesn't need more reactive managers.
It needs **builders. Steady hands. Quiet giants.**

It needs people who come into a space—whether broken, average, or thriving—and leave it *better* than they found it.

That's your job.
And it always will be, no matter what store, team, or company you're with.

• • • • •

Better doesn't always mean dramatic.
It doesn't always mean awards or recognition or some Instagrammable moment of "turnaround."

Sometimes better looks like:

- A new hire who was ready to quit but stayed because someone finally trained them
- A backroom that runs without you having to check it every day
- A shift lead who learned to coach because you let them
- A toxic behavior that no longer shows up
- A team that doesn't flinch when you're off the floor

These are the real wins.
This is the legacy.

· · · · ·

I've left stores with clean metrics and high sales—but no real impact.

And I've left stores that had more to fix—but the team was *solid*.
The foundation was there. The habits were there. The trust was there.

And I walked away proud.

Not because everything was perfect.
But because I knew I didn't just show up—I built something.

· · · · ·

"You're not measured by how you lead when things are easy.
You're remembered for what you leave behind when you go."

· · · · ·

So when your time comes to hand over the keys—whether it's to a new manager, a new team, or a new season of life—ask yourself this:

- Did I leave it better than I found it?
- Did I build people?
- Did I protect standards?
- Did I speak up when others stayed silent?
- Did I serve, teach, and lead with intention?

- Did I help this place become stronger, even in small ways?

If you can say yes?

You did the job right.

• • • • •

Leadership in retail isn't always glamorous.
But it is meaningful.

Every table you teach someone to fold.
Every difficult conversation you handle with grace.
Every person you lift up instead of push down.

That's what matters.

That's what stays.